Robert Griffin III

By Jon M. Fishman

AMAZING ATHLETES

⌐ Lerner Publications Company • Minneapolis

Lerner Publications Company
A division of Lerner Publishing Group, Inc.
241 First Avenue North
Minneapolis, MN 55401 U.S.A.

Website address: www.lernerbooks.com

Library of Congress Cataloging-in-Publication Data

Fishman, Jon M.
     Robert Griffin III / by Jon M. Fishman.
        pages   cm. — (Amazing athletes)
     Includes index.
     ISBN 978–1–4677–1878–3 (lib. bdg. : alk. paper)
     ISBN 978–1–4677–1895–0 (eBook)
     1. Griffin,Robert, III, 1990-2. Football players—United States—Biography—Juvenile literature.
  3. Quarterbacks (Football)—United States—Biography—Juvenile literature. I. Title.
  GV939.G775F57 2014
  796.332092—dc23 [B]   2012048539

Manufactured in the United States of America
1 – BP – 7/15/13

TABLE OF CONTENTS

Robert Griffin III is one of the most exciting young quarterbacks in football.

NEW TEAM LEADER

Washington Redskins quarterback Robert Griffin III looked down the field. A New Orleans Saints **defender** rushed toward him. Robert had only a second to decide where to throw the football.

Robert and the Redskins were playing their first game of the 2012 National Football League (NFL) season. New Orleans had the lead, 7–3. Robert was a **rookie**. He wanted to show that he could be a star in the NFL. But the Saints are a good team. They won the Super Bowl in 2010. New Orleans quarterback Drew Brees is one of the best in the game.

Drew Brees throws the ball down the field. Brees played for the San Diego Chargers before joining the Saints in 2006.

Robert fired a pass over the middle of the field. Redskins **wide receiver** Pierre Garcon reached up and snagged the pass out of the air. Garcon ran past defenders for an 88-yard touchdown! Washington took the lead, 10–7.

The long touchdown was just Robert's seventh pass in the NFL. And he knew it was too early to celebrate. Brees and the Saints were not going to give up.

Robert throws the ball to Pierre Garcon.

Robert celebrates his first NFL victory with fans.

Washington got the ball back. Robert drove the team down the field again. This time, he threw a five-yard touchdown pass to Aldrick Robinson. The Redskins increased their lead to 17–7.

The Redskins kept putting up points. **Running back** Alfred Morris scored two touchdowns. The team kicked four **field goals**. Brees tried to keep his team in the game. But he couldn't keep up with Robert and the Redskins. Washington won the game, 40–32. Robert's first NFL game was a victory!

"Robert did an unbelievable job to play the way that he did in his first game in the National Football League," Redskins coach Mike Shanahan said. Even better, Washington was off to a great start in 2012. Would they be able to keep it up?

Coach Shanahan knows that Robert has a chance to be great.

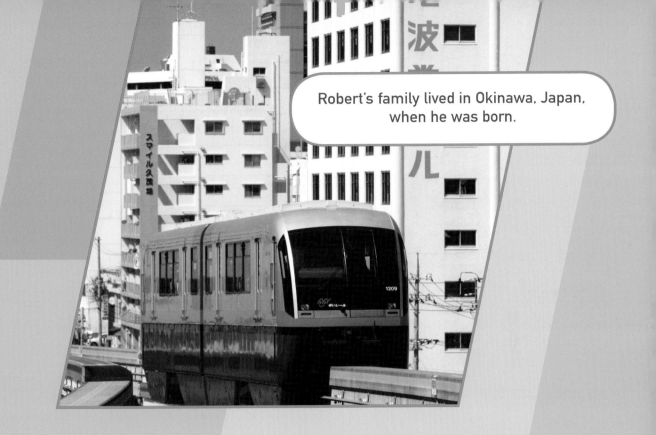

Robert's family lived in Okinawa, Japan, when he was born.

ARMY KID

Robert Lee Griffin III was born on February 12, 1990, in Okinawa, Japan. His family called him Robby. His mother and father, Jacqueline Griffin and Robert Griffin Jr., were members of the U.S. Army. Robby has two older sisters, Jihan and De'Jon.

Robby and his family moved a lot when he was young. After Japan, the Griffins were assigned to an army base in the state of Washington. When Robby was six, the army moved the family again. This time, Robert Jr. and Jacqueline were sent to South Korea. Robby and his sisters moved to New Orleans, Louisiana, to live with their father's family.

Robby had never lived in a city as large as New Orleans. He had to get used to a new school and new friends. Some of the kids teased Robby about his long hair. They called him Ponytail.

"I think it was a good experience for Robby," said his mother, "because he got to see a side of life he had no idea about." Robby's parents returned to the United States after one year. They moved the family to Fort Hood, Texas.

By third grade, it was clear to Robby's family that he would be an athlete. "He was already out throwing the [football] every day," said his father.

But football wasn't the only sport that interested Robby. He told his father that he wanted to be the next Michael Jordan.

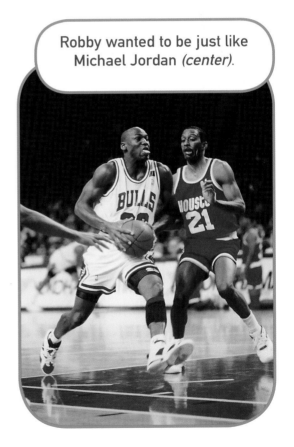

Robby wanted to be just like Michael Jordan *(center)*.

Robby's father made his son dribble a basketball with his left hand for an hour. Then Robby told his father that he wanted to be the fastest boy on the army base. Robert Jr. made his son run up hills with a car tire tied to his back.

"I was mad," said Robby about the way his father pushed him to work hard. "Then I realized what it was going to take. My dad would say, 'If you're going to do something, why not be the best?'"

Robby's father served in Iraq during the Iraq War (2003–2010) with soldiers like these.

BECOMING A LEADER

February 12, 2003, was a big day for Robby. It was his 13th birthday. It was also the day he learned that his father was leaving the family to spend six months in Iraq. Robby cried when he heard the news. He knew his father would be in danger.

Robby *(left)* learned a lot from his father *(right)*.

On March 19, 2003, the United States declared war on Iraq. "A lot of kids [at Fort Hood] had parents who didn't come back," said Robby. "I didn't want to be one of those kids. But I knew that if [my father] didn't come back, I was going to have to take care of my family."

Robby grew up a lot while his father was in Iraq. He knew his family was counting on him. He continued to work hard, as his father had taught him.

Robert Jr. returned safely home from Iraq after six months. He and his son didn't talk about the war. They talked about football.

In 2004, Robby played on the freshman football team at Copperas Cove High School in Copperas Cove, Texas. He moved up to the **varsity** team for his sophomore season. But Robby mostly sat on the bench behind the team's senior quarterback.

Robby *(right)* was hard to bring down even in high school.

Robby was a fast runner on the track as well as the football field.

By his junior year in 2006, Robby was a star on the school's track team. He was also the starting **point guard** on the basketball team. Robby still found time to study. He almost always got straight As on his report cards.

Robby won the starting quarterback job in 2006. He was a good fit as the fastest runner in school. But his father knew that the best quarterbacks throw first and run second. He wanted his son to try to throw the ball more often.

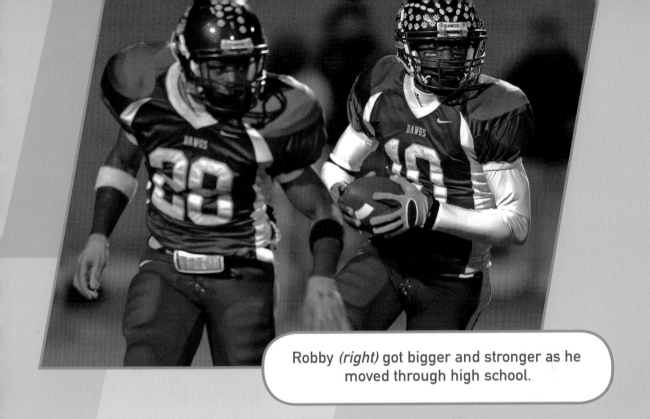

Robby *(right)* got bigger and stronger as he moved through high school.

BECOMING A STAR

Robby took his father's advice to heart. He threw the ball whenever he could and only ran when he had to. The style paid off in Robby's first year as the starting varsity quarterback at Copperas Cove.

Robby threw 25 touchdown passes in 2006. He ran for eight more touchdowns. He threw only two **interceptions** all season. Robby was just as good as a senior in 2007. He threw 16 touchdown passes and ran for 24 more.

Colleges around the country wanted Robby for their football teams. But most teams wanted him to play wide receiver or **defensive back**. University of Houston coach Art Briles thought Robby could be a good college quarterback. Coach Briles had seen Robby throw at a football camp. "I looked at our coaches and said, 'Fellas, we've got something special here,'" said Briles.

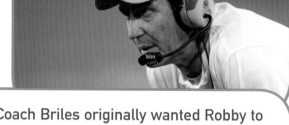

Coach Briles originally wanted Robby to play football at the University of Houston.

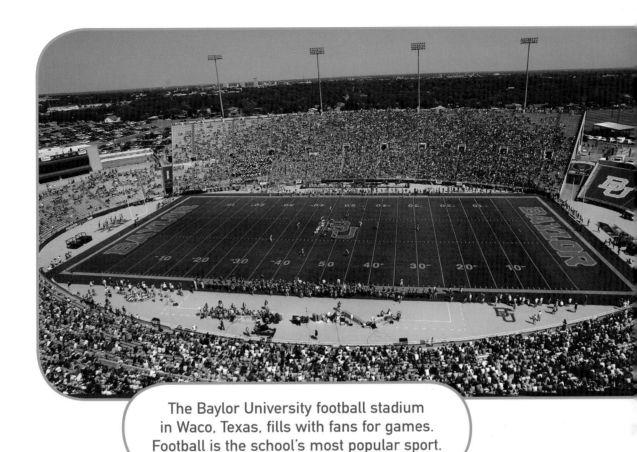

The Baylor University football stadium in Waco, Texas, fills with fans for games. Football is the school's most popular sport.

Coach Briles left Houston to become the coach at Baylor University before the 2008 season. Robby decided he would join the Baylor Bears too. The school wanted Robby to play quarterback. They also had a good track team.

Robby played well during his first college game even though his team lost.

Robby's first college game was against Wake Forest University. Coach Briles put Robby in the game in the second quarter. Baylor lost, but Robby showed that he could be a star. People on campus began calling him RG3.

Baylor finished the 2008 season with just four wins and eight losses. But RG3 gave the team hope for the future. The young quarterback threw 15 touchdowns with only three interceptions in 2008. He ran for 13 more touchdowns.

RG3 also starred on the track team in 2008. He ran a career-best time in the 400-meter **hurdles** to win the Big 12 **Conference** championship.

RG3 just missed running at the Olympic Games in Beijing, China, in 2008. He tried out for Team USA but missed the cut.

Baylor began the 2009 football season with a win and a loss. Then disaster struck in the team's third game. RG3 fell to the field in the first quarter. His knee was hurt. But he kept playing and threw three touchdown passes before leaving the game at halftime. Doctors later told RG3 that he had torn a **ligament** in his knee.

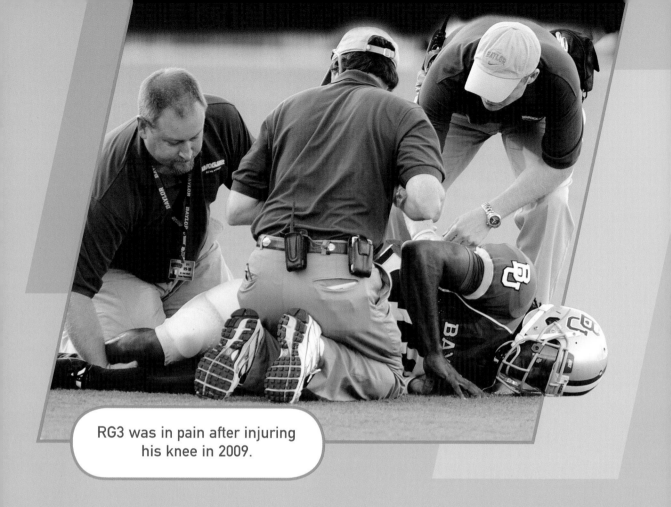

RG3 was in pain after injuring his knee in 2009.

CAPITAL QUARTERBACK

RG3 had surgery on his knee. He missed the rest of the 2009 football season. He decided to give up track. He wanted to be sure to be ready for football in 2010.

RG3's knee healed in time for the 2010 season. He was as good as ever. He threw 22 touchdown passes and ran in eight more. Even better, RG3 led the Bears to their first bowl game since 1994. They faced the University of Illinois in the Texas Bowl. Illinois came out on top, 38–14.

RG3 throws a pass after returning to football in 2010.

RG3 had one of the greatest seasons for a quarterback in college football history in 2011. He threw for 37 touchdowns and ran for 10. After one game against Kansas State University, he asked his girlfriend Rebecca to marry him. She said yes.

The Bears won nine games in 2011 and went to the Alamo Bowl. They beat the University of Washington, 67–56.

After the Alamo Bowl, people began wondering about RG3's future in the NFL. He was sure to be one of the top picks in the 2012 **draft**. Most people thought either RG3

RG3 celebrates after winning the Alamo Bowl.

or Stanford University's Andrew Luck would be chosen first.

The Indianapolis Colts chose Luck with the first pick in the draft on April 26, 2012. The Washington Redskins quickly took RG3 with the second pick.

RG3 was excited to have a new home. He still remembered when teams thought he would be a better wide receiver than a quarterback.

RG3 won the Heisman Trophy in 2011 as the most outstanding player in college football.

The NFL Draft is held each spring.

RG3 *(center)* poses at the NFL Draft with his family after being chosen by Washington.

"A team finally fell in love with me," RG3 said. "They want me for who I am, and I can't wait to go play for them."

The Redskins named RG3 their starting quarterback before the start of the 2012 season. He led the team to a 10–6 record, but they lost to the Seattle Seahawks in the first round

RG3 runs for a touchdown in 2012.

of the playoffs. Overall, it was a good year for the young quarterback. But RG3 hurt the ligaments in his knee again. He had surgery as soon as the season was over. He'll be ready to go again in 2013.

Washington last won the Super Bowl in 1992. But with RG3 leading the way, they might be back in the big game soon.

He knows he must work hard in the NFL and be a good teammate. "It's not a matter of talent or how far you can throw it," RG3 said. "It's all about who you are as a person."

A Washington fan holds a sign showing RG3's face. The team has hope for a better future with RG3 leading the way.

Selected Career Highlights

2012 Named Washington Redskins starting quarterback
Chosen with the second pick in the NFL draft

2011 Won the Heisman Trophy
Named National Player of the Year by *Sporting News*
Led Baylor to victory in the Alamo Bowl

2010 Named Big 12 Offensive Player of the Year
Named Big 12 Comeback Player of the Year
Started all 13 of his team's games after knee surgery in 2009

2009 Missed most of the season with a knee injury
Threw four touchdown passes and zero interceptions
Named Big 12's Best Athlete by *Sporting News*

2008 Was the youngest college starting quarterback in the country
Named the Big 12 Freshman of the Year by *Sporting News*
Won the Big 12 championship in 400-meter hurdles

2007 Ranked among the nation's top 20 high school quarterbacks by
Texas Football Magazine
Rushed for 1,285 yards and threw for 1,356 yards
Won the Gatorade Texas Boys Track & Field Athlete of the Year
award

2006 Rushed for 876 yards and threw for 2,001 yards

Glossary

conference: a group of college football teams. The Big 12 Conference includes schools such as Baylor University, Texas Tech University, and the University of Texas.

defender: a player whose job is to stop the other team from scoring

defensive back: a football player who tries to prevent wide receivers from catching passes

draft: a yearly event in which professional sports teams take turns choosing new players from a selected group

field goals: successful kicks between the U-shaped poles at both ends of a football field. A field goal is worth three points.

hurdles: a race in which runners jump over barriers

interceptions: passes caught by the opposing team's defense. When a defensive player intercepts a pass, that player's team gets control of the ball.

ligament: a short, flexible band that connects two bones

point guard: a player on a basketball team who is responsible for running the team's offensive plays

rookie: a first-year player

running back: a football player who runs with the ball

varsity: the top sports team representing a school

wide receiver: a football player who catches passes

Further Reading & Websites

Fishman, Jon M. *Andrew Luck*. Minneapolis: Lerner Publications Company, 2014.

Kennedy, Mike, and Mark Stewart. *Touchdown: The Power and Precision of Football's Perfect Play*. Minneapolis: Millbrook Press, 2010.

Savage, Jeff. *Drew Brees*. Minneapolis: Lerner Publications Company, 2011.

The Official Site of the National Football League
http://www.nfl.com
The NFL's official website provides fans with the latest scores, schedules, and standings, and biographies and statistics of players, as well as the league's official online store.

Sports Illustrated Kids
http://www.sikids.com
The *Sports Illustrated Kids* website covers all sports, including the NFL.

Washington Redskins: The Official Site
http://www.redskins.com
The official website of the Washington Redskins that includes the team schedule and game results, late-breaking news, team history, biographies of players such as Robert Griffin III, and much more.

Index

Photo Acknowledgments

The images in this book are used with the permission of: © Ronald Martinez/Getty Images, pp. 4, 6, 19, 29; © Chris Graythen/Getty Images, p. 5; © Jason Schulz/Dreamstime.com, p. 6; © John David Mercer/USA TODAY Sports, p. 7; AP Photo/Aaron M. Sprecher, p. 8; © iStockphoto.com/GA161076, p. 9; © Jerry Coli/Dreamstime.com, p. 11; © John McDonnell/The Washington Post via Getty Images, p. 14; AP Photo/Eric Gay, p. 15; Image of Sport Photos/Newscom, p. 16; AP Photo/Steve Traynor, p. 17; © Stephen Dunn/Getty Images, p. 18; © Brian A. Westerholt/Getty Images, p. 20; AP Photo/Waco Tribune Herald/Rod Aydelotte, p. 22; © Thomas Campbell/USA TODAY Sports, p. 23; Cal Sports Media via AP Images/Patrick Green, p. 24; © Chris Chambers/Getty Images, p. 25; © Al Bello/Getty Images, p. 26; © Rob Carr/Getty Images, p. 27; © Jonathan Newton/The Washington Post via Getty Images, p. 28.

Front Cover: © Rob Carr/Getty Images.

Main body text set in Caecilia LT Std 55 Roman 16/28.
Typeface provided by Adobe Systems.